Do What
The F**k I Say

Do What
The F**k I Say
Sebastian Melmoth II

Illustrated by Catherine Denvir
Designed by Rebecca Jezzard

EBURY
PRESS

3 5 7 9 10 8 6 4 2

Published in 2013 by Ebury Press, an imprint of Ebury Publishing

A Random House Group Company

Text © Sebastian Melmoth II 2013

Sebastian Melmoth II has asserted his right to be identified as the author of
this Work in accordance with the Copyright, Designs and Patents Act 1988

The Random House Group Limited Reg. No. 954009

Addresses for companies within the Random House Group can be found at
www.randomhouse.co.uk

A CIP catalogue record for this book is available from the British Library

The Random House Group Limited supports The Forest Stewardship Council® (FSC®),
the leading international forest certification organisation. Our books carrying the
FSC label are printed on FSC® certified paper. FSC is the only forest certification scheme
endorsed by the leading environmental organisations, including Greenpeace.
Our paper procurement policy can be found at **www.randomhouse.co.uk/environment**

Illustrations: Catherine Denvir
Designer and Typesetter: Rebecca Jezzard
Production: Caroline Rush

Printed and bound by Butler, Tanner & Dennis

Set in Museo Sans Rounded

ISBN 9780091957186

To buy books by your favourite authors and register for offers, visit:
www.randomhouse.co.uk

"The old believe everything;
the middle-aged suspect everything;
the young know everything."

— Oscar Wilde

I know all your friends have an iPad,
With zillions of thingies to play,
But you'll just have to wait until Christmas
And do what the fuck I say.

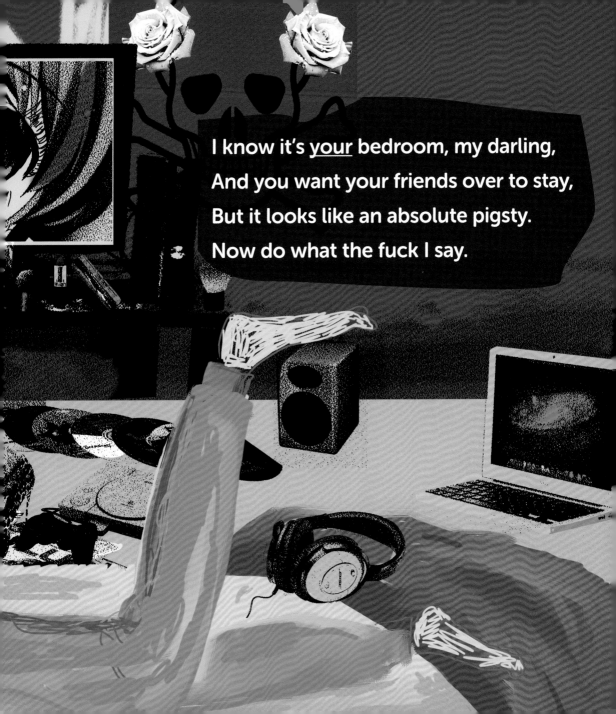

I know it's <u>your</u> bedroom, my darling,
And you want your friends over to stay,
But it looks like an absolute pigsty.
Now do what the fuck I say.

Yes, you've told us you're soon going vegan
To live upon lentils all day,
But 'til then, pass your father the gravy,
Please do what the fuck I say.

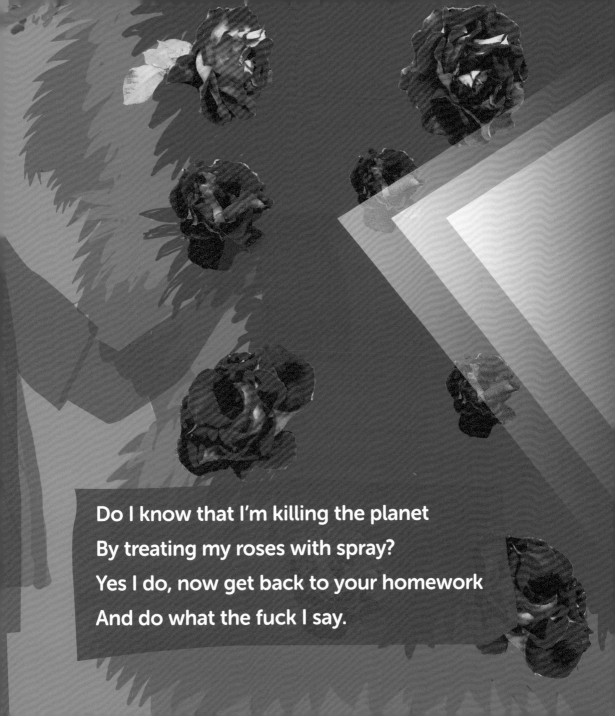

Do I know that I'm killing the planet
By treating my roses with spray?
Yes I do, now get back to your homework
And do what the fuck I say.

No I don't want you top of your class, dear,
Or *summa cum* bleeding *laude*,
But second from bottom's pathetic,
Why not do what the fuck I say?

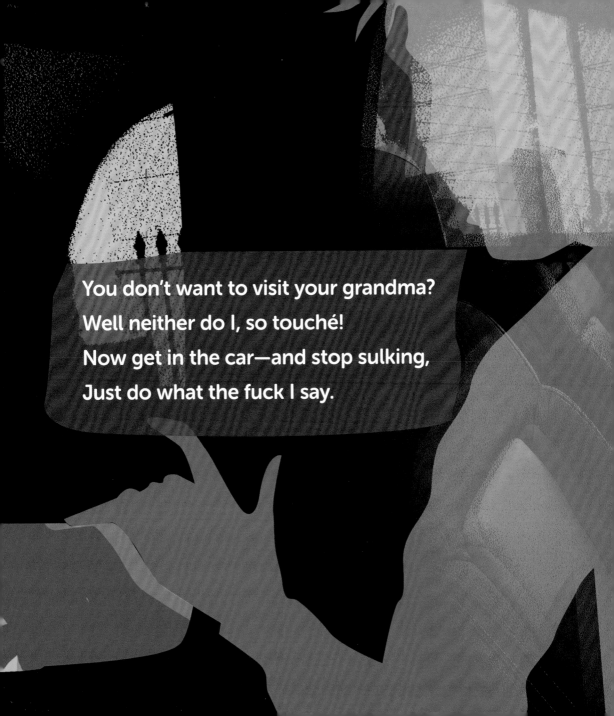

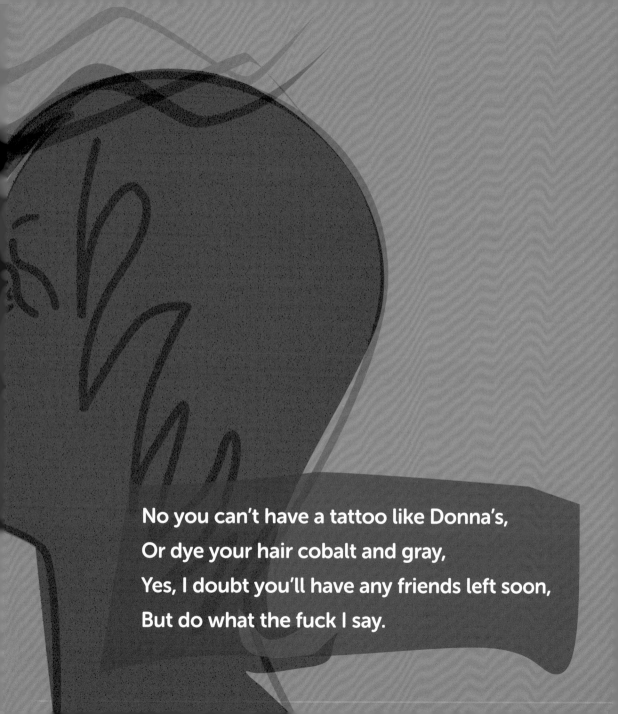

No you can't have a tattoo like Donna's,
Or dye your hair cobalt and gray,
Yes, I doubt you'll have any friends left soon,
But do what the fuck I say.

I know perfectly well what I sound like
When I order a café au lait,
But this 'bourgeois old fart' is your parent,
So just do what the fuck I say.

I've seen what you've posted on Facebook
And it comes down this minute, OK?
No we're not going to have a discussion,
Just do what the fuck I say

No you're not sleeping over at Zara's,
I've heard that her folks are away.
Never mind how I know—you're not going!
You'll do what the fuck I say.

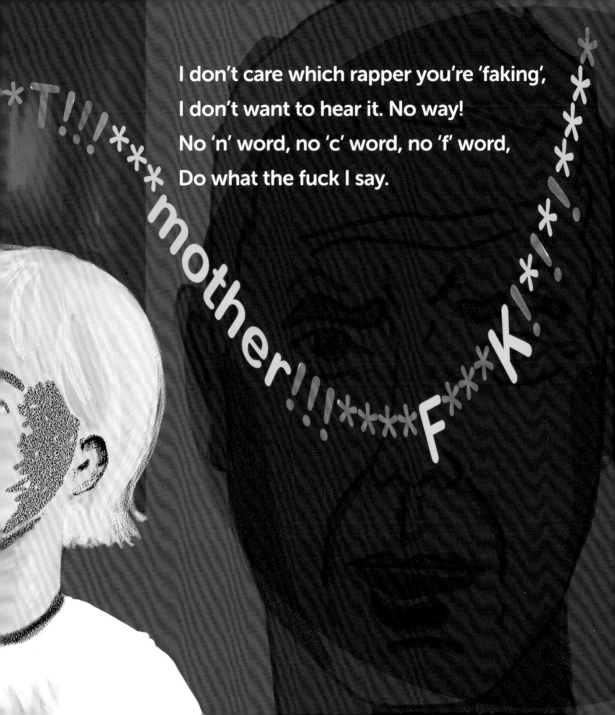

I don't care which rapper you're 'faking',
I don't want to hear it. No way!
No 'n' word, no 'c' word, no 'f' word,
Do what the fuck I say.

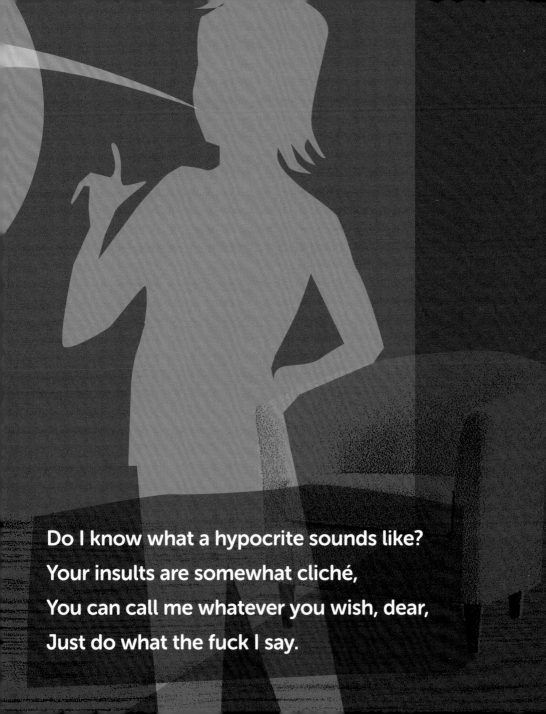

Do I know what a hypocrite sounds like?
Your insults are somewhat cliché,
You can call me whatever you wish, dear,
Just do what the fuck I say.

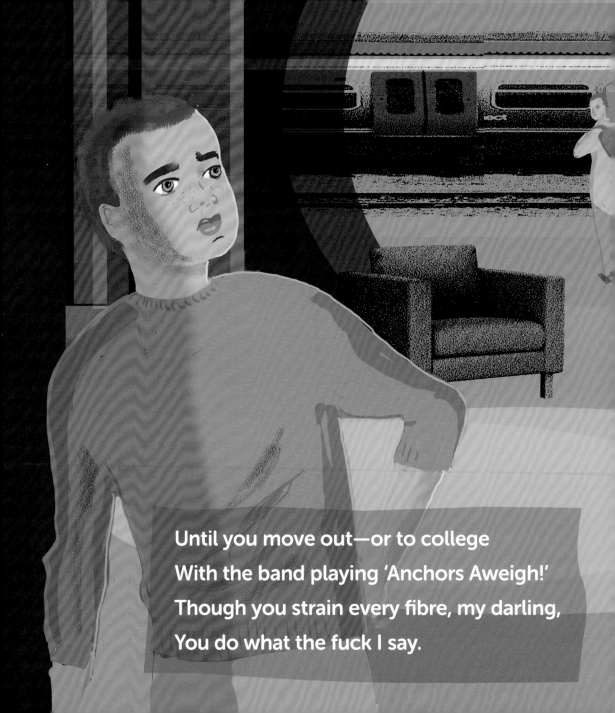

Until you move out—or to college
With the band playing 'Anchors Aweigh!'
Though you strain every fibre, my darling,
You do what the fuck I say.

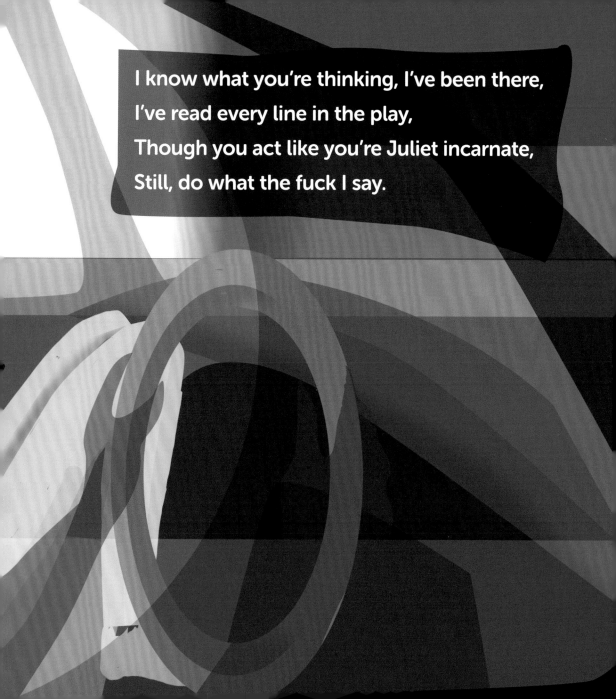

I know what you're thinking, I've been there,
I've read every line in the play,
Though you act like you're Juliet incarnate,
Still, do what the fuck I say.

No you're not going to 'bum out all summer
Rehearsing to be a deejay',
You're getting a job—and that's final,
You'll do what the fuck I say.

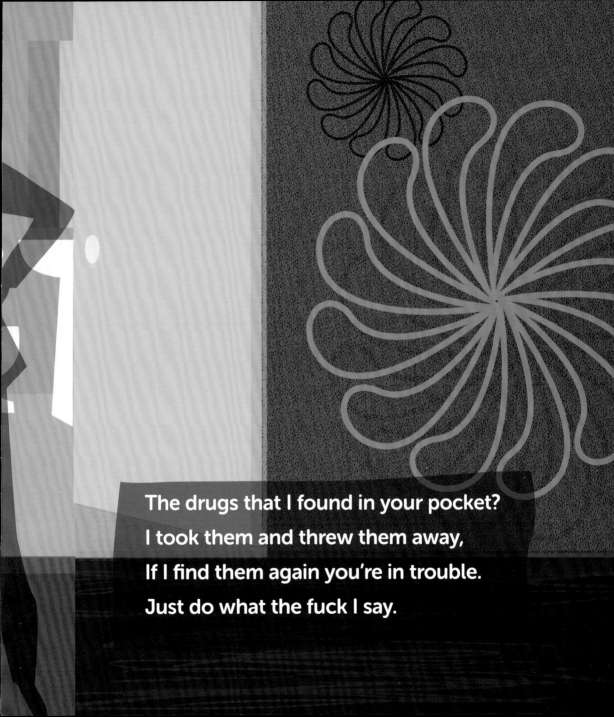

The drugs that I found in your pocket?
I took them and threw them away,
If I find them again you're in trouble.
Just do what the fuck I say.

Have sex if you must, but not here dear.

Do I care if you're straight or you're gay?

No I don't, but you're using a condom!

Please do what the fuck I say.

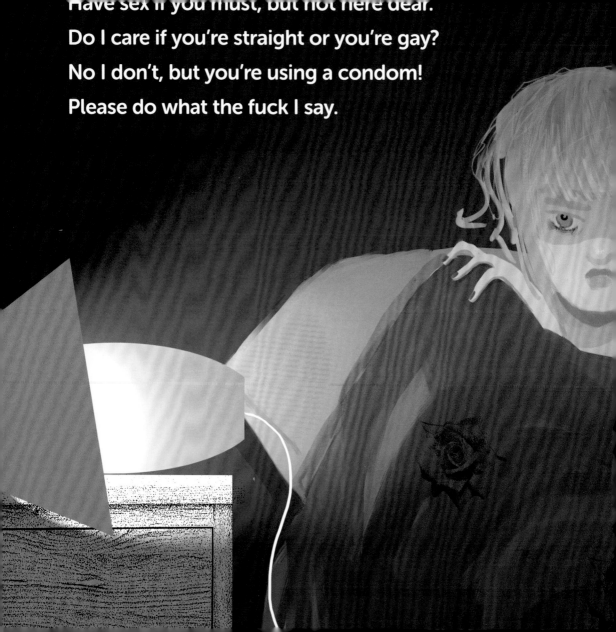

One day you'll have kids of your own, dear,
And though you'll be busy, I pray
You'll spare me a thought as you're yelling,
'Do what the fuck I say!'

The End.

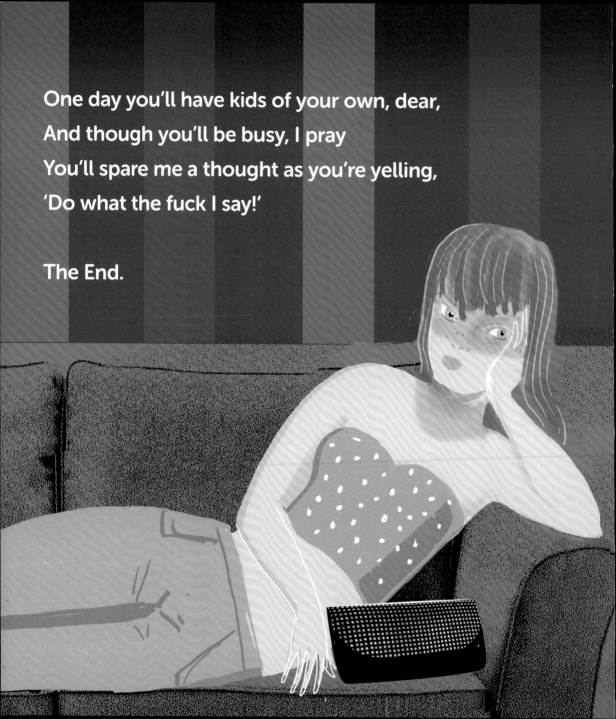